Virtual Apprentice

AUTHOR

By Gail Karlitz

Checkmark Books®
An imprint of Infobase Publishing

Virtual Apprentice: Author

Checkmark Books
An imprint of Infobase Publishing, Inc.
132 West 31st Street
New York, NY 10001

ISBN: 978-0-8160-7548-5

The Library of Congress has cataloged the hardcover edition as follows:

Library of Congress Cataloging-in-Publication Data

Karlitz, Gail.
  Virtual apprentice. Author / Gail Karlitz.
     p. cm.
  Includes index.
  ISBN 978-0-8160-6756-5 (hc : alk. paper) 1. Authorship – Vocational
guidance – Juvenile literature. I. Title.
  PN153.K37 2007
  808'.02023 – dc22
                            2006036584

Checkmark Books are available at special discounts when purchased in bulk quantities for businesses, associations, institutions, or sales promotions. Please call our Special Sales Department in New York at (212) 967-8800 or (800) 322-8755.

You can find Ferguson on the World Wide Web at http://www.fergpubco.com

Produced by Bright Futures Press (http://www.brightfuturespress.com)
Series created by Diane Lindsey Reeves
Interior design by Tom Carling, carlingdesign.com
Cover design by Salvatore Luongo

Photo Credits: Table of Contents Pamela Moore: Page 5 McPherson Colin/CORBIS SYGMA; Page 7 Stefano Bianchetti/CORBIS; Page 8 Bettmann/CORBIS; Page 12 Reuters/CORBIS; Page 15 Ariel Skelley/CORBIS; Page 18 Pamela Moore; Page 20 YinYang; Page 23 Bettmann/CORBIS; Page 24 Dieter Hawlan; Page 28 Linda and Colin McKie; Page 31 Karen Struthers; Page 32 Tim Graham/CORBIS; Page 35 Stephen McSweeny; Page 53 Katie Ambrose.

Note to Readers: Please note that every effort was made to include accurate Web site addresses for kid-friendly resources listed throughout this book. However, Web site content and addresses change often and the author and publisher of this book cannot be held accountable for any inappropriate material that may appear on these Web sites. In the interest of keeping your on-line exploration safe and appropriate, we strongly suggest that all Internet searches be conducted under the supervision of a parent or other trusted adult.

Printed in the United States of America

Bang PKG 10 9 8 7 6 5 4 3 2 1

This book is printed on acid-free paper.

CONTENTS

Welcome to the World of Authors

Dorothy and Toto in the Emerald City of Oz,
Harry, Ron, and Hermione at Hogwart's School,
Tigger, Piglet, and Eeyore in the Hundred Acre Wood,
Peter, Wendy, and the Lost Boys in Neverland…

All of these are places that are as real to

us as any place we've actually been, people who are more real to us than many who live and breathe today. As different as all these worlds may be, they have one thing in common. They all come from wildly popular children's books created by imaginative authors.

What about you? Do you daydream a lot? Do you like to make up stories about the people and events around you? Do you enjoy telling friends about your favorite sports or hobbies? Do you like learning about famous or incredibly interesting people?

If any of these thoughts sound familiar to you, if you are constantly making up stories or keeping journals, if you think there is nothing better than a good book…then you may have what it takes to be an author, and this is the place to find out how to make it happen.

What is it really like to be an author? Read on, and find out about

- what being an author is all about

- what authors do each day (and, yes, it's a lot more than sitting at a desk and typing)

- the trends in today's books and the technologies that are changing the way authors write, produce, and even read books

- what real authors have to say when kids like you ask them what it's *really* like to be an author

Finally, spend a day as a "virtual author" and see if you have what it takes to see your words (or worlds) in print!

Are you ready to take over where Harry Potter author J.K. Rowling left off?

CHAPTER 1

A Way with Words

FUN FACTOID

The Bibles that Johannes Gutenberg printed in 1455 sold for 300 florins each—about what a clerk would earn in three years. That was very expensive, some say comparable to the cost of buying a car today. Even at that price, though, it was still a lot more reasonable than a handwritten Bible that could take a single monk 20 years to transcribe, and was more comparable to the cost of a house today.

Imagine describing a book to people who have never seen one. Where would you begin? How could you explain the way a good book can pull you in with exciting words, enticing pictures, great characters, and riveting plots? What could you say to help them understand how important books are to so many people—from the youngest child to the oldest adult? How could they understand how indispensable books can be as ways to relax, to escape the stresses of our usual days, to stretch our imaginations, and to learn about things we are interested in?

Books can be for children, teens, or adults. They can be fiction (drawn from an author's imagination) or nonfiction (based on history, facts, or opinions). Books can be made up of words alone, words and pictures, or just pictures. They can have scenes or characters that pop up in three dimensions, flaps with pictures or words hidden under them, different textures to touch, and even patches to scratch-and-sniff.

People have been telling each other stories ever since the first cave dwellers told about their hunts or explained the world around them through the adventures of imaginary gods and goddesses. Eventually, stories were written

"A writer gets more knowledge, and if he's good, the older he gets, the better he writes."
– MICKEY SPILLANE, CRIME WRITER

Authors everywhere owe a debt of gratitude to Johannes Gutenberg, inventor of the world's first printing press.

down, first with hieroglyphics carved into stone tablets (a little too heavy for most people), then on papyrus, parchment, and silk scrolls (too expensive for all but the royals), and finally on paper (which took a long time to copy by hand).

It wasn't until the 1400's that Johannes Gutenberg changed the world by finding a way to use moveable metal type to print

Theodor Geisel, otherwise known as "Dr. Seuss," is still one of the world's most famous children's authors.

on paper. It took a while to get from Gutenberg's early efforts to where we are today, but he started the chain that made it possible for people in almost every corner of the world to have access to books. No wonder Gutenberg has been called one of the most influential and important people in history.

Recipe for a Fiction Book

Authors do have a wealth of choices in what they write about, but there are a few things that really have to be included in their books. Of course, the recipe for a fiction book is not exactly the same as the recipe for a nonfiction one.

Fiction books have to include a plot (the story), characters (the people who are in the story), and one or more settings (the places where the action occurs). Fiction books may also include dialogue (the specific words that the characters say or think).

Where do authors get ideas for the plots of their books? From just about any place. Many authors base their stories on something they have experienced. Or wish they had experienced. Or heard about someone else experiencing. Some start with a plan for the whole book. Some start with an ending and work back to a beginning. Author R.L. Stine says, "Almost all my ideas come from thinking of a really good title and seeing where that leads. I work backwards from every other author; most authors get an idea for a story and think of a title later."

Although the plot is important, even the best plot in the world will not make for a good book if the characters aren't interesting to read about. As Bonnie Bryant, author of The Saddle Club books, says, "The characters are the single most important part of a story. If the characters aren't real, believable, and compelling, nobody's going to care what happens to them and what they do about it."

Authors have to know everything about the characters they create, even more than what they share with their readers. They have to know their characters so well that they can predict what each character will do in any situation. And authors have to be accurate about their characters. If a character is a pilot, the author needs to know everything about how people become pilots, what pilots do, and even some of the words pilots use when they are flying or preparing to fly.

With the plot and the characters in place, authors then make choices about the settings for their stories—where and when the actions take place. The setting can be a real place—for example a mystery that takes place in Disney World or New York City—and may include references to real streets, restaurants, and stores. It can be totally imaginary—like a science fiction adventure on Mars. It can even be a blend of both—an imaginary place based on a real one—perhaps an adventure that takes place in a huge museum that is a lot like many different real museums. In fiction books, characters can travel to the furthest points on Earth, to other planets, or through time. Or they can do no traveling at all,

FUN FACTOID

In 1954, some people thought that many children were not learning to read because the books used in the schools were boring. When Dr. Seuss was asked if he could write an interesting book using no more than 250 basic words, he created *The Cat in the Hat* using only 225 different words. In 1960, a friend bet Dr. Seuss that he couldn't write a book with only 50 words. That challenge resulted in *Green Eggs and Ham*.

with the whole book taking place in a house, a school, or an airplane. A story can happen in the present, the past, or the future. It's all up to the author.

Authors have to know as much about their settings as they do about their characters. They must be careful that everything makes sense for the location and time in which the action takes place. So that means no cell phone for the knight in shining armor and no snow storms in a Disney World mystery!

The Facts About Nonfiction

Nonfiction books have a very different recipe. They need to have a subject (the topic of the book), and facts or opinions about that topic. Nonfiction books may also include a bibliography (a listing of where the author got the information for the book) and an index (a section in the back of the book that enables readers to find information they are looking for within the book).

There are almost no limits to the subjects for nonfiction books. They can be about history, current events, or biographies. They can include instructions for building furniture or advice on anything from fixing automobiles to raising children (or learning what it's really like to be an author!). Nonfiction books can be poetry, cookbooks, joke books, or journals. They can have interviews, quotations, photographs, diagrams, or opinions.

There are so many topics available for nonfiction authors, and there are so many different people who want to learn about different things, that many more nonfiction books are published each year than fiction. In fact, in 2005, there were almost 130,000 new nonfiction books and only 21,000 new fiction books.

Art, or illustration, is the final ingredient for both fiction and nonfiction books, especially those written for children. In fact, for children's books, the expression "A picture is worth a thousand words" is a real understatement. Pictures and colors make books appealing to young children. They also give meaning to words, concepts, and emotions that young children may not yet understand. Seeing a picture of a "red ball" helps them connect the idea of "red" with the actual color and the word "ball" with those round things they like to throw. Without the illustrations, half the "story" would be missing.

CHECK IT OUT

Did you know that many of the names in the Harry Potter books indicate something about the title character? You can check it out at "What's In a Name?" at http://www.theninemuses.net/hp.

Who Wrote What?

Can you match these authors with the book or series they are most known for?

1 J. M. Barrie
2 Maurice Sendak
3 C.S. Lewis
4 Peggy Parish
5 A. A. Milne
6 H. A. Rey
7 Beverly Cleary
8 Eric Carle
9 Gary Paulsen
10 L. Frank Baum

A Amelia Bedelia
B Where the Wild Things Are
C Hatchet
D The Chronicles of Narnia
E The Very Hungry Caterpillar
F Curious George
G Peter Pan
H Ramona
I The Wizard of Oz
J Winnie the Pooh

ANSWERS: 1-G, 2-B, 3-D, 4-A, 5-J, 6-F, 7-H, 8-E, 9-C, 10-I

The Ups and Downs of Life as an Author

Authors, like people in most professions, have their professional "up times" and "down times." Authors usually feel excited and rewarded when their books get published, when they get good reviews, and when lots of people read them. And then there's the public recognition and the many different awards for authors and illustrators. The ceremonies may not be huge, televised events like the Oscars or the Grammys, but they are just as important to the people who receive the awards. Everyone likes to be recognized for good work, and awards in any industry usually translate into more sales, more dollars, and more future projects.

The most well-known awards for children's books are

• The Caldecott Medal is awarded to the artist of the most distinguished American picture book for children.

As first lady, Laura Bush, a former librarian, has often shared her love of books with children.

• The Newbery Medal goes to the author of "the most distinguished contribution to American literature for children."

• The Corretta Scott King Award recognizes an African-American author and an African-American illustrator whose works "encourage and promote" world unity and peace and serve as an inspiration to young people.

• The Theodor Seuss Geisel Award recognizes the author(s) and illustrator(s) who have made the biggest contribution in the area of "beginning reader books" published in the United States.

As for the "downside" of an author's life–being an author means learning to live with lots of rejection. Even the most successful authors have been through the rejection experience. Although he is famous now, Dr. Seuss' first book was rejected by 26 publishers; Norman Bridwell, who created Clifford the Big Red Dog, was turned down by 15; and almost every publisher in the U.S. declined to publish J.K. Rowling's Harry Potter books. Finding the right publisher for their books is every author's greatest challenge.

Show Me the Money

Of course, making money is another "upside" of an author's life. Just as with actors, artists, musicians, and other people in the arts, some authors are able to support themselves with their writing, others write as a side job while making their living doing something else, and a few become very wealthy superstars.

So how do authors make money from their work?

Authors usually get hired by publishing companies in one of two ways. The publisher, or an editor working for the publisher, may hire an author on a *work-for-hire* basis. In that situation, the author agrees to write a book for a specified amount of money. The author then receives that amount, no matter how many copies of the book are sold. More often though, authors work on a *royalty* basis, and get a percentage of the sales of the book. The more copies of the book that are sold, the more money the author makes.

Royalties are calculated as an agreed percent of the price printed on the cover of the book, multiplied by the number of books that are sold. Let's say you write a paperback book that has a cover price of $6.95. If your royalty rate is 6%, you will get almost 42 cents for each book sold. If the book sells 10,000 copies, you will earn $4,170. If the book sells 100,000 copies, you will earn $41,700. And if it sells a million copies, you earn $410,700!

One problem with the royalty system is that authors need to live while they are writing the book and while it is being produced before the sales are made. So, they usually get some money when they make the agreement with the publisher and when they finish writing. This money is called an *advance*. Publishers pay royalties to their authors twice a year after their books are published, but payments do not begin until the book has earned enough to cover the advance.

Does all this information about writing different types of books get you even more interested in being an author? Do you think you have what it takes to add some more treasures to the millions of books that have already been written? Do you still want to learn more about what authors do? Well, you're in the right place.

FIND OUT MORE

Look up the past winners of awards for children's literature at http://www.childrensbooks.about.com/od/awardwinners. How many of these books have you read?

CHAPTER 2

Author at Work

FUN FACTOID

"Small Sam" and **"Puny Pete"** were some of the names Charles Dickens tried for the character of the sick little boy in *A Christmas Carol* before he settled on **"Tiny Tim."** Scarlett O'Hara, the main character in *Gone With the Wind,* was originally named **Pansy.**

Writing books, especially books for kids, sounds like an easy job. After all, there have probably been a few times when you left your language arts homework for the very last minute and wrote an entire story in less than an hour. A book is longer, so you figure you should be able to crank one out in a few days or so. Then you can just sit back for a while, and write another one next week. Right?

Wrong! There's a lot more to it than most people realize.

Put yourself in this imaginary author's shoes for a day and see for yourself.

A Typical Author Day

Being a full time author is a real job and today is a workday. Like many authors, you have several books going at once. You are most famous for your Percy books, a series for very young children. You are also planning a series for eighth graders.

Your plan for today includes

• publicizing *Percy's Perfect Party*, the most recently published book in the series

• working on *Percy's New Puppy*, an upcoming book for the series

"You never know where your next idea will come from. It's always fun to see how one thing leads to another."

—DIANE LINDSEY REEVES, AUTHOR

Finding inspiration for your next book.

• fine-tuning ideas for the next six books in the Percy series

• talking to your editor about your ideas for your new book for eighth graders

It is going to be a really busy day, so you get up at 7:00 a.m., hoping to get in some writing time before everything else starts happening. You shower, dress, and have breakfast. Sure, no one will care if you don't do any of those things, but you've already learned that when you act like you're going off to a job, you feel more professional about the whole day and make more progress. Although, since it's your home office, you set the "dress code." Translation: jeans and a T-shirt are "professional attire" here.

By 7:30 a.m. you're at your computer. First things first–how is *Percy's Perfect Party* doing? You do a quick Internet search to see if there have been any more newspaper or magazine reviews, then hop over to Amazon.com to see how the sales are going. Yes! It's up in the rankings from yesterday. That is double good news: more readers are enjoying your books and more sales mean more royalties for your bank account. Way to go!

Time to get back to the book you're working on today. You check the detailed outline you and your editor have agreed on. You're up to the chapter about how Percy teaches his new puppy to walk on a leash. Oops…it's been a long time since your own dog was a puppy. Do you train a puppy to walk on your left side or your right? Does it even matter? You don't even remember how long the training sessions should be or how many times a day. Back to all those puppy-training books you bought before you started this book. You definitely don't want to give your readers the wrong information about puppy training.

You're going strong on the leash training section when you remember that you have a radio interview scheduled for 9:00 a.m. Time to shift mental gears. The host of "Raising Responsible Kids," a radio show in Tulsa, Oklahoma, wants you to talk about *Percy's Perfect Party*. They like the way your book uses a fun story and delightful illustrations to help parents make sure that their young children's parties are safe and appropriate for their age. They really like how you show Percy and his sister helping to prepare for the party and making sure that all of their guests are comfortable and have a good time.

FIND OUT MORE

Copy editors (sometimes called proofreaders) check a manuscript for errors in style, punctuation, grammar, and spelling. Most copy editors use the same symbols to tell the author what to change. You can find the standard symbols and abbreviations in the back of most dictionaries or online at http://www.ccc.commnet.edu/writing/symbols.htm. Use these symbols whenever you review an early draft of your next writing assignment at school.

Climbing to the Top

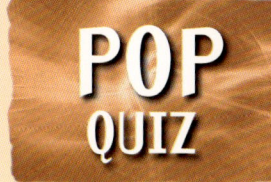

POP QUIZ

Many of the most successful authors had to overcome major challenges in their lives. See if you can match the person with the situation.

1 He had a writing disability that caused him to reverse letters and misspell words. Thinking that he was just sloppy and inattentive, his teachers told him that he would never be able to write. He had to rewrite all his novels at least 25 times but, as he says, "I liked what I wrote."

2 Born in Austria, he was always rebellious. At the age of 16, while working in his uncle's resort hotel, he shot the hotel's headwaiter during an argument. His family gave him a choice: go to reform school or go to America.

3 He was born in Los Angeles when "it had more horses than automobiles and more jack rabbits than people." He went to four different colleges but never graduated from any. Although he wrote many fiction and nonfiction books for adults, he wrote his first children's book when he was 60. He wrote 25 more books for young people, before he died at 91.

4 She was one of the worst readers in her school and almost didn't make it to second grade.

5 He was a miserable student, flunked the ninth grade, and finally graduated from high school with, as he says, "probably a D-average." His parents drank and argued, and he found safety in a library, where he fell in love with reading. He did any kind of job to earn money and even ran away with a carnival at 14. He wrote 100 books by the time he was 50.

6 When she was seven years old, she knew she wanted to be an author and that everything in her life could contribute to her writing. She said, "When my father would yell at me, I told myself someday I'd use it in a book."

7 After high school, he spent 13 years putting doors on big cars in a Michigan automobile factory. While doing that job, he began work on his award-winning book.

A Paula Danzinger (Amber Brown)

B Gary Paulsen, (Hatchet)

C Christopher Paul Curtis (Bud, Not Buddy)

D Avi, (Crispin: The Cross of Lead)

E Beverly Cleary (Ramona)

F Scott O'Dell (Island of the Blue Dolphins)

G Ludwig Bemelmans (Madeline)

ANSWER: 1-D, 2-G, 3-F, 4-E, 5-B, 6-A, 7-C

Authors spend lots of time working in front of a computer.

You murmur a quiet "hurray for technology!" to yourself. Radio interviews are important–they help make people aware of your books. (And more sales mean more royalties!) But traveling all that way for an interview would not be a smart use of your time. Fortunately, technology makes it possible for you to sit at your desk and sound just like you are in the studio a thousand miles away. And your office outfit still works just fine!

Your interview is done by 9:30, and it's back to work. It takes a little while to get back into the groove of your young audience, but soon you're rolling again until 11:30, when you get a reminder from your computer that the illustrator you work with is coming to show you her sketches of the new puppy that will be the model for the current book. And she's bringing lunch with her–another reason to look forward to the visit.

The illustrator presents several different ideas for the puppy. She already knows that it can't be just any old puppy. Percy's new puppy has to look like the kind that won't grow up to be bigger than he is (no St. Bernard pup for this book!). It has to be cute, not scary. Not too fancy looking. Not something that's inappropriate for five-year-old Percy. You think back to the problems that came up after the *101 Dalmatians* movie, when so many families with little kids rushed out to get a cute dog like the ones in the movie. Unfortunately, they didn't check to find out that Dalmatians have too much energy and are too difficult to train for most kids to handle. A lot of stressed-out families resulted from that movie! Anyway, very young Dalmatians don't even have their spots yet–not at all what you're looking for in your book.

You and the illustrator agree on the sketches that you think will be just the kind of puppy Percy would have. When the illustrator leaves you head back to your computer for some more writing. You check your outline to make sure you've included everything about leash training. You read over everything you've written. Are the words too hard for the kids who will be reading this story? Are there too many, or too few, words for the page? Have you overused any one or two particular words? Does the chapter flow easily from the previous one?

Right in the middle of this, your editor calls. She wants an update on your progress on the next set of Percy books. For the past three months, you've read every parenting magazine and child-raising book

Character Sketch

Create a character that you'd enjoy reading about. Here are some things you can include in your description. You can probably think of many more!

> What does your character look like –height, weight, hair, posture?

> What kind of clothes does he or she like to wear?

> What's in his pocket or her purse?

> What does he or she like to do after school?

> What does he or she want for a birthday gift?

> How many brothers, sisters, and pets does your character have?

> Describe your character's best friend.

you could lay your hands on. You're pretty confident that you've decided on the topics the next six books have to deal with, and you share those thoughts with your editor. She is enthusiastic, and you promise to get her some outlines soon.

You decide that since everything is going so well, this would be a good time to tell your editor about your new series for older readers. The books are going to be about a family who has just moved from a big city to a small town because of a change in the father's job. The central character, a middle school girl, is not happy about the move. She's even less happy when she starts at her new school and learns that everyone in town thinks that the previous owners of her new house were just a little bit strange, that no one knows where they are now, and that before you moved in, some very strange things seemed to be happening on that street. You are very well prepared to talk to your editor about this idea. You've already worked out most of the other characters –the younger sister and brother, the parents, the best friend from the city, and the students in the new school. You've spoken to about 50 middle school students, and you've gotten lots of ideas for plots for the books. You've written some sample chapters to

FUN FACTOID

Authors also spend time reading mail from their readers. Ann Martin (Baby-Sitters Club) gets more than 15,000 fan letters a year. Tomie dePaola (Strega Nona) gets more than 100,000.

Even the best authors sometimes get writer's block.

show how the books will include many common tween problems and experiences, how some of the characters will bring a smile to the readers' faces, and how the dialogue will be true to middle-school-age life. You cross your fingers, take a deep breath, and start telling your editor all about the new idea. Guess what? She loves it! She wants to see the sample chapters right away. You are having a triple-header super amazing day!

By 3:00 p.m. it's time to change into a slightly nicer outfit and head off to the bookstore in the mall. You're going to be reading *Percy's Perfect Party* to their afternoon children's reading club, and then autographing copies that people buy. There are a few reasons you like to do these readings. Sure, they do sell books, and it's nice to make money. But, more importantly, you get to meet the kids who are reading your stories. You see how they respond to different parts, what they especially like, and whether they have questions because you may have left out some detail. You see if they laugh where you didn't intend to be funny. Or don't laugh where you thought you were extremely funny. And you get ideas for future books.

You're home by 5:00, just in time to watch some kids' shows on TV. It helps to keep up with what they're watching–you get a sense of what they like, you get reminded about the level of their sense of humor, and you don't seem totally clueless the next time you talk to a group of kids.

By 7:00, you've been at work for almost 12 hours. You've spent less than four hours actually writing, and you've completed most of one page. It's time to call it a day. Maybe tomorrow you'll have more time to write…if you hadn't already scheduled a trip to be the guest author of the day at a school two hours away!

CHAPTER 3

Writing Tech and Trends

FUN FACTOID

Many authors find that they work better using the "old fashioned" methods. J.K. Rowling wrote all of the Harry Potter books in longhand. Ann Martin recently gave in to the computer. Her early Baby-Sitters Club books all started out with pen and paper.

It's usually pretty easy to tell this year's fashions from last year's. Maybe a certain color combination is "hot" this year. Or last year's jeans were all baggy; this year's are straight legged or bell-bottomed. Last winter everyone wore zippered hoodies; this winter it's pullover sweatshirts (with no hood). Trends, or changes in styles, are easy to see in things like clothes or shoes. Did you know that there are trends in books as well? And that it's important for authors to know about changing trends so that they can write books that people will want to buy?

There are some books, especially children's books, that have been around forever and will probably always be around, no matter what the current trend. *Goodnight Moon* is one of those. Written by Margaret Wise Brown, it was first published in 1947, has sold more than 11 million copies, and is still a favorite. *The Very Hungry Caterpillar* is still a bestseller with more than 22 million copies sold since 1969. Other longtime favorites include *The Tale of Peter Rabbit* (1902), *Winnie-the-Pooh* (1926), *Madeline* (1939), *Make Way for Ducklings* (1941), and *Charlotte's Web* (1953).

> "Those of us who write do it because there are stories inside us burning to get out."
> —JUDY BLUME, AUTHOR

Changes for Young Readers

The very earliest books for children were intended to do two things–teach kids how to read, and teach them moral lessons. Books for very early readers were often limited to the alphabet and to prayers. Books were meant for lessons, not for fun. You probably figured that much out by now, haven't you?

Once upon a time, before computers were invented, authors like Agatha Christie prepared their manuscripts using typewriters.

Technology makes working from home a reality for many publishing professionals.

The trend in children's books changed a lot when Lewis Carroll first published *Alice's Adventures in Wonderland* in 1865. *Alice* was the very first children's book that was intended for pleasure and did not have any morals or lessons for its readers.

The trend in children's books changed again when Dr. Seuss wrote *To Think I Saw it on Mulberry Street* in 1937. That was the beginning of a new kind of book for children—a book that could be fun, or silly, or from the child's point of view. In 1957, Dr. Seuss totally changed the look and feel of "easy reader" books with *The Cat in The Hat*. Although it only used easy, beginning words, the book told a story that was fun, and had characters who weren't "perfect children."

The important thing for authors is that books for beginning and more advanced readers have continued to take new risks and create new trends. The books are more "real" than they used to be. Stories are told from children's, rather than an adult point of view. Characters are from many different races. Mothers are doctors, or lawyers, or other workers. Fathers cook, clean house, and take care of babies. Stories are set in cities rich and poor, in different countries, and in rural areas, not just in perfect looking suburbs. Families are different too. Some children live with a grandparent, or only one parent. Sometimes there is divorce, death, or illness. Each year, children's books (as well as adult books) show more of what life can be for different people. And books that are written purely in the old style just won't sell. Just like last year's style of jeans.

Other Trends

Look around a bookstore. Do you see any trends in the new book section? Before the Goosebumps series, there were few scary books for kids. When those books became popular, scary books for kids suddenly appeared everyplace. Have you noticed the influence of the huge success of Harry Potter? Suddenly, books that feature wizards, magic, and amazing creatures are making frequent appearances in the children's book section. The success of a movie can also inspire a new trend in books. What do you see happening today?

Another recent trend is the rise of graphic novels. These stories, presented in comic book form, have become increasingly popular among adults, teens, and children. At first teachers and parents were afraid that these books would make children less interested in reading, but the opposite seems to be happening. According to an article in the *School Library Journal*, junior high school (or middle school) libraries that included comics had almost twice as many student visits, and students read many more non-comic books as well. Graphic novels are even being used in the classroom for students with short attention spans. Even old favorites, like the Baby-sitters Club series, are being redone in this format.

No one could have predicted the amazing success of Goosebumps, Harry Potter, or graphic novels. You can bet that there will be another incredible new trend by the time you are ready to be a full-fledged author. Just hope you're the one to identify it and those royalty checks will start adding up quick!

High- and Low-Tech Tools of the Trade

Most of the tools that authors use to do their work are considered common and not very technical. On the very low-tech end, there's good old pen and paper. You probably don't give a lot of thought to the ballpoint pens you use, but they were a very big deal when they first came out. Fountain pens, as the earlier types were known, used liquid ink, which you kept in a bottle on your desk. Hmmm…bottle of liquid ink plus messy desk, full of papers and notes plus hurried author, or curious cat, or exploring child. What do you think happened to many manuscripts? Not to mention furniture, clothes, and rugs. The ballpoint pen seems like an easy and obvious solution, but it was far from that. It took 61 years from the time the first model was developed in 1888 until it was good enough to sell to the public in 1949. People clearly liked this new pen since stores sold more ballpoints than fountain pens in the very first year.

The big news before the ballpoint pen was the typewriter, invented in 1867. It made writing a lot faster. And it was great for authors who didn't have the best handwriting. The only problem was that it wasn't very easy to fix mistakes or make changes–which usually meant retyping the whole page.

The biggest news of all–more important to all of us than the ballpoint pen or the typewriter–is the computer. If you've grown up in the age of the computer, you might find it hard to list all the benefits that came along with it. We can get our thoughts down on paper quickly and then easily add to them, subtract from them, or even move entire sentences or paragraphs with just a few keystrokes. We no longer need to have a dictionary or thesaurus on hand, or go through everything a few dozen times to make sure we didn't miss any misspellings. We can emphasize some words by putting them in bold or italics or different fonts.

Computers certainly make it easier for authors to write. The incredible bonus that comes along with computers today is the Internet. Can you even imagine what life was like B.I. (Before Internet)? Remember that night you sat down to finish your research paper at 10:00 p.m.? Not too many years ago, you would have been out of luck. The library would have been closed by the time you thought about going or, if you did go earlier, there was a good chance that you would not have found a book with the

FUN FACTOID

Mark Twain was the first author to submit a typewritten manuscript (*Life on the Missis-sippi*) to a publisher. Mark Twain bought the typewriter in 1874 when he saw someone demonstrate that she could type more than 50 words per minute. He later was convinced that he had been tricked. As much as he practiced, he could never do more than 19 words per minute.

information you needed. What about the report you had to do on the war in Iraq? The Internet makes it possible to follow the action as it happens, to find maps of the locations that are in the news, and to see pictures of the cities and buildings that are affected. You can even check on current weather conditions any place in the entire world!

The Internet provides information that even the best libraries cannot. You can read interviews and biographies of just about any author you can think of; you can even see what most of them look like!

Authors can use the Internet to do research that would have been impossible before. They can find out information on just about any topic for a nonfiction book. In fact, they can even see if a book they have in mind to write has already been written! For fiction books, the Internet makes it a breeze to have all the details as realistic as possible –street names, restaurants, and even travel times between different cities. The Internet has also created a whole new way for people to relate to each other. Readers can write to their favorite authors, and authors can learn what their readers think. Authors can join on-line groups that critique each other's writing, or find the best publisher or literary agent.

And, in addition to everything else, the Internet lets authors listen to their favorite music while they work or play a few games of computer Scrabble when they need a break. Gutenberg's printing press was certainly a good thing for readers and writers, but it definitely couldn't keep you entertained while you worked!

The High Tech Side

Technology has also radically changed the way people read and publishers produce books. In today's world, books are not just ink on paper. E-books are electronic versions of books that can be downloaded from the Internet or borrowed from a library. You

E-book List

Project Gutenberg—does that name ring a bell?—is a group of volunteers who put books into formats to "encourage the creation and distribution of eBooks." There are 18,000 free books in the Project Gutenberg Online Book Catalog and another 50 are added each week. About 2 million e-books are downloaded each month. The project uses books whose copyrights have expired, or obtains written copyright permission for all books in their catalogue. Check them out at http://www.gutenberg.org. Are there any books you might like to read?

FIND OUT MORE

need a handheld device to read them–a special e-book reader, a cell phone, or a personal organizer.

There are some real advantages to e-books. Want to find something specific? Just do a search instead of thumbing through the pages. Want to take a bunch of books with you? About 500 books can be stored on one CD. Too dark to read? Just get a backlit reading device (one that has a light source that shines from the back of the image toward the viewer). The bad news is that reading e-books can be really hard on the eyes. Some people think they can actually damage eyes. And it's really hard to curl up in a big comfy chair with an electronic device.

A New Way to Produce Books

Some authors choose to print and market the books they write themselves, or self-publish. Those authors like the idea of being completely independent, with no editor to tell them to make changes, and no sales force to keep them to certain dates. They also like not having to share the profits earned from their work

Some experts predict that technology will someday replace printed books.

with a publisher. However, self-publishing means that the author has to not only do the author's job, he or she also has to do the publisher's job too. Publisher's typically take care of the many details involved in taking an author's typewritten pages and turning them into finished books—editing, designing, illustrating, and printing. They also market the books and distribute them to the places who want to sell them and the people who want to buy them. So, while many enterprising authors find great success in self-publishing their own work, many others find themselves overwhelmed by the enormity of the task.

One of the things that has made self-publishing possible is the development of print on demand, or POD. Print on demand is a new way to produce books, using digital printing.

Print on demand is a production process, and it costs much less than traditional printing, especially if there are not too many books involved. The reasoning behind it is very similar to the reasoning behind digital printing of photographs.

If you wanted to print your own photos, you could use regular film and build a photo processing plant. You would need lots of space for your plant, many machines, an assortment of papers and chemicals, and some people to run everything. That would not be a good investment if you only wanted to print one or two rolls of film each month. For Kodak or Fuji, who print millions of pictures each year, that kind of investment makes a lot of sense. Once they have set up the plant and printed a few hundred thousand photos, it costs little to print another couple rolls.

In the past, you would have been stuck, unable to print your own pictures. Now, though, you can use a digital camera and print one, two, or 10 pictures whenever you want.

Print on demand (POD) is a digital process that works the same way. No need for printing presses and other equipment, inks, or huge bolts of paper. No need for a lot of employees to run the process, to pay for the paper and printing for books that may not sell, or maintain a warehouse to store all the books that are waiting to be sold. Just print out the books as you need them. Many bigger publishers are also using print on demand processes to keep copies of their older titles (called their "backlist") available longer.

REALITY CHECK

Having technology is a good thing; being proficient with it is even better. See how fast you can type. Go to http://www.calculatorcat.com/typing_test and take a free typing test.

CHAPTER 4

Author in Training

CHECK IT OUT

The Harry Potter books have many different covers. Check them out at the Cover Art Gallery at http://www.factmonster.com/spot/harry gallery.html. Why do you think the versions of the covers are so different?

Have you wondered why people decide to become authors? It's probably not for the fame and fortune! Most authors are not as well-known or as highly regarded as movie stars or television celebrities. Very few authors have fan clubs–although sometimes the characters from their books do. Many authors do have their own Web sites though.

For most authors, writing is something that they just *have* to do. Just listen to what some well-known authors have said. Gloria Steinem, who writes adult nonfiction, said, "Writing is the only thing that, when I do it, I don't feel I should be doing something else." Isaac Asimov, author of 270 books said, "I write for the same reason I breathe–because if I didn't, I would die." Dr. Asimov was so determined to write, that he declared, "If the doctor told me I had six minutes to live, I'd type a little faster."

Getting Started as an Author

There are almost as many ways of getting started as there are authors. Some authors know what they want to do from a very young age. They start writing when they are young, for themselves or for school and local magazines. Many go to college

"Life is my college. May I graduate well, and earn some honors!"
– LOUISA MAY ALCOTT (LITTLE WOMEN)

One thing that almost all authors have in common is an early love of reading.

and major in English, literature, or journalism, then head out to work for a magazine or a publishing company.

Other authors fall into writing almost by accident and find that it is their real love. And some authors begin with one type of writing and find their true calling in another.

Back in the "old days," it wasn't very important to have a formal education to be a writer. Some of the best-known writers,

Often, famous people like Sarah Ferguson, the Duchess of York, write books.

including Mark Twain, Louisa May Alcott, and Charles Dickens, had very little formal education. Today, though, things are very different, and it would be very hard to become an author without a college education.

Formal Education

Although a college degree is almost a requirement for writers, it won't guarantee you a slot on the best-seller list a week after graduation. It won't even guarantee that you will have a book published a week (or year, or five years) after graduation. As you've probably seen by now, there's a lot more to writing a successful book than meets the eye. Colleges offer the opportunity to major (or specialize) in English, literature, journalism, writing, and many even more specialized areas.

There's a lot to learn in the college classroom. Students have the chance to try out different styles, to write a lot more, to get feedback from instructors and other students, and to see what others are writing, and learn from that as well.

And then there's the high tech side of writing. When your parents were your age, most people thought that computers were for the math and science majors, not for the creative folks who wanted to be writers. Although we can't be sure about what writing will be like a few years from now, many colleges are already teaching their writing students the skills needed to write for Web sites or electronic publications. Some schools even encourage future authors to learn about graphic design, audio, video, and 3-D animation, all skills that may be as important in a few years as the ability to type is today.

College offers the opportunity to learn outside of the classroom as well. As they say, the best way to write is to write from your own experiences and college is the place to build up a big supply of experiences. College can provide the chance to meet people from different places, to live and study in another coun-

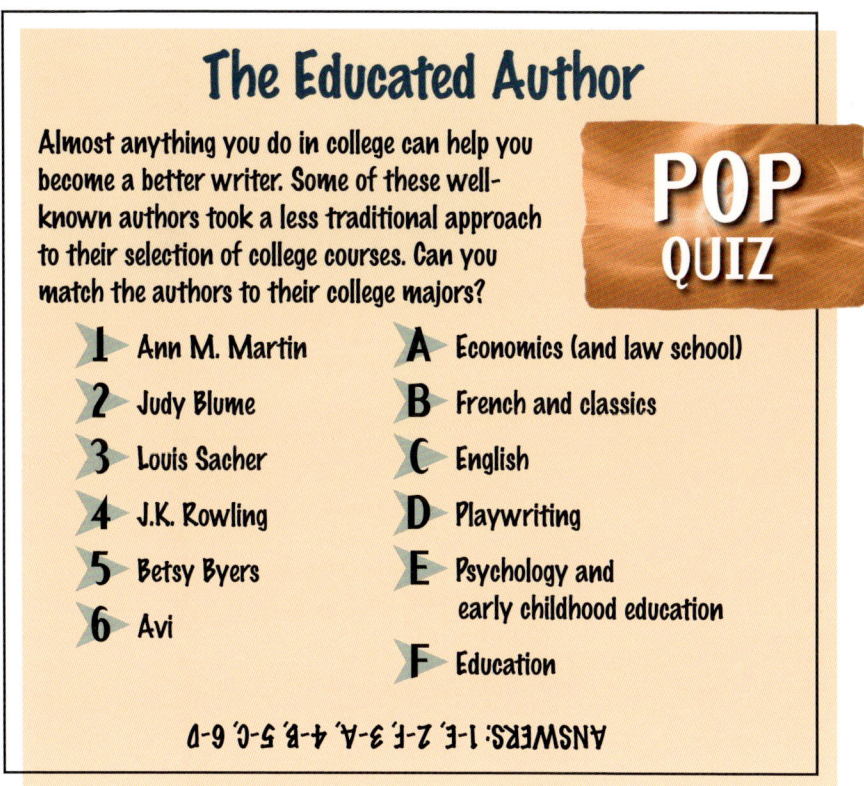

The Educated Author

POP QUIZ

Almost anything you do in college can help you become a better writer. Some of these well-known authors took a less traditional approach to their selection of college courses. Can you match the authors to their college majors?

1 Ann M. Martin
2 Judy Blume
3 Louis Sacher
4 J.K. Rowling
5 Betsy Byers
6 Avi

A Economics (and law school)
B French and classics
C English
D Playwriting
E Psychology and early childhood education
F Education

ANSWERS: 1-E, 2-F, 3-A, 4-B, 5-C, 6-D

try, and to learn about how people think, learn, and behave. Some colleges provide opportunity to have classes or special meetings with published authors, and many help students get summer jobs or internships (short term trial jobs) in the publishing business.

Finally, college helps you to get on the road toward your goal. The authors you most admire probably started with a job in publishing, education, or some similar field. And what do you need to get a job in those fields? Right! A college education.

Personal Traits Count Too

Check out the authors of the books that are popular today. How many of them are younger than 20? Younger than 25? 30? How old were the authors of your favorite books when they did their writing? It's no coincidence that very few authors are published when they are relatively young.

Writing is not like getting a driver's license. There's no official "minimum age." But it does take a while to build up the life experience that makes for a good author.

Talent is important for becoming an author. But talent alone is not enough. As author Bruce Coville says, "Talent is only part

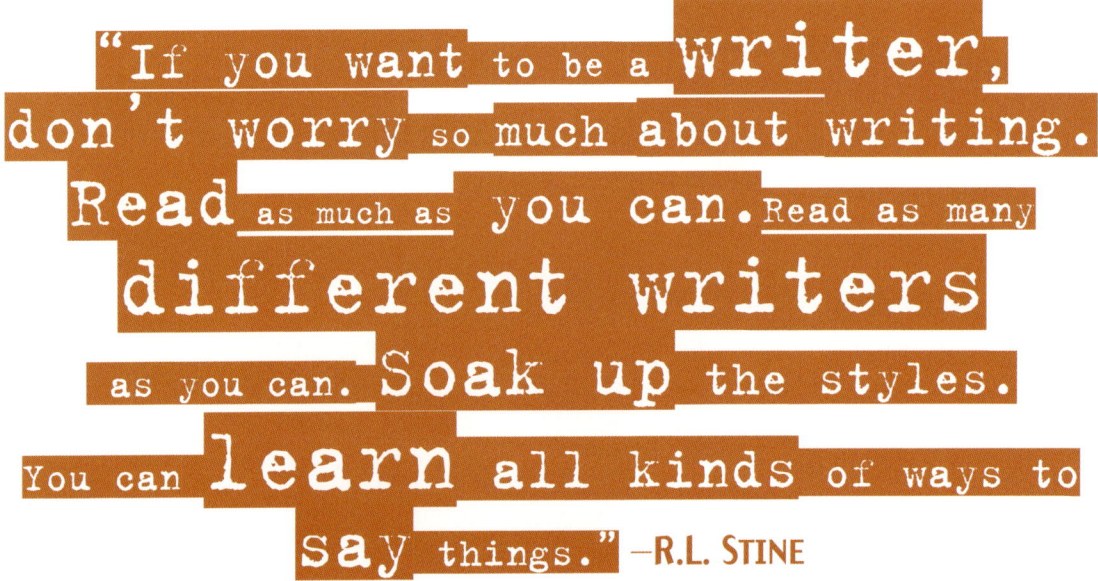

"If you want to be a writer, don't worry so much about writing. Read as much as you can. Read as many different writers as you can. Soak up the styles. You can learn all kinds of ways to say things." —R.L. STINE

Authors tend to be very curious about the world around them.

of what it takes to be a writer. Luck and courage and mostly just plain old sticking to it are just as important."

The tips that successful authors offer almost always involve the traits of persistence, patience, and practice. Let's take a look at what those three words mean on the path to becoming an author.

Persistence: All authors get rejections. Even successful authors have new ideas rejected. The key is to hang in there. Bruce Coville also reminds us, "…and most important of all—never give up. You must believe in yourself, even when no one else does. People will think you are crazy. They will think you are conceited. You will get discouraged. You will think it is hopeless. You will think you are never going to get your work published. And if you give up, that will be true. You must believe in yourself, and never give up."

Young Authors

FIND OUT MORE

There are many organizations that are looking for material from young writers. Here are just a few of them.

▶ Amazon.com and other booksellers accept book reviews from teen writers.

▶ NextSTEPmag.com Teen Writing Contest (for nonfiction essays) at http://www.nextstepmagazine.com/nextstep/teen-contests.aspx

▶ Stone Soup magazine (writing and art for ages 13 and under) at http://www.stonesoup.com

▶ Writer's Digest Your Assignment for Kids competition (for ages 13 and under) at http://writersdigest.com/contests

▶ Teen Ink: A Magazine and Book Series Written by Teens for Teens http://www.teenink.com

See if your school participates in these writing programs (or if they would consider participating).

▶ The Writing Conference, Inc. Contest http://www.writingconference.com/contest.htm

▶ The Scholastic Art and Writing Awards http://www.scholastic.com/artandwritingawards

Patience: It's easy to think that the "superstar" authors can just sit down and write a book. Don't believe that for a minute! Books take a lot of work, and authors need to have a lot of patience–mostly with themselves.

Authors have to do a lot of rewriting before they are happy with what they have written. Louis Sacher, author of *Sideways School* and *Holes,* says, "You have to be willing to rewrite. I didn't become a good writer until I learned how to rewrite. And I don't just mean fixing spelling and adding a comma. I rewrite each of my books five or six times, and each time I change huge portions of the story." J.K. Rowling rewrote the first chapter of her first Harry Potter book 10 times before she was happy with it. And *The Cat in the Hat*, which looks like such a simple book, took nine months to write! Dr. Seuss probably didn't realize how big a challenge it was when he agreed to write a children's book with only 225 words. *Make Way for Ducklings*, Robert McCloskey's classic book, with a total of 1,152 words, took a whole year to write. The ducklings he was using as models weren't very cooperative about posing for the sketches, and the author had to be very creative about slowing them down.

Practice: There's no arguing with the fact that the professional athletes we watch are all talented and just plain good at what they do. Yet, they practice almost every day between games as well as in the off-season. What they know is that athletic skills can disappear quickly when they are not practiced often. The same is true for writing skills. As author Caroline B. Cooney says, "Learning to write is exactly like learning a musical instrument or a sport. You have to practice every day if you want to become good at it. There are no shortcuts."

Getting Started Now

Okay, if you want to be a writer, you have to go to college and then you have to work at something else for a few years to get some life experience. Does that mean that you can't do anything toward your goal for the next few years? Absolutely not!

You've already taken a big step by reading this book and doing the activities in it. But there are many more things you can do now.

The one thing that professional authors constantly advise young people to do is to read, read, read! Some authors think that reading is even more important than writing. Read all kinds of books by all kinds of authors.

When you're not reading, you can work on your writing skills. To become a better writer (and to develop your practice trait), look for opportunities to write and get feedback. Start right in your own school by taking as many writing classes as you can. Seek out other opportunities in your school by joining the newspaper, literary magazine, or yearbook staff. Then look in your community. Many libraries, community colleges, and even adult education programs sponsor young writer's workshops.

Build up your life experience inventory too. Many things that happen in your life right now will seem more interesting a few years in the future. As long as you don't forget them! Keep a journal, and write every day, about your experiences, thoughts, or observations. You never know what will lead to a book idea!

Practice Makes Perfect

Look for programs where you can practice your writing skills. Some places to start include

➤ The National Book Foundation's Summer Writing Camps at http://www.nationalbook.org/writingcamp.html

➤ Other summer programs at specialized camps or on college campuses are listed at http://www.mysummercamps.com.

Take a chance on submitting your writing wherever you can. See if your local newspaper accepts submissions. Look for organizations that sponsor writing contests for young people.

CHAPTER 5

Book Work

Literally dozens of people are involved in the transformation from a vague idea in an author's mind to an actual book in a reader's hands. If you love books, there are many ways to make them part of your life's work. You may find some of these other job ideas interesting as possible career opportunities. Or, like many other authors, you may find them useful stepping stones to your writing career.

Acquisitions Editor

Do you think you can recognize a good book when you see one? Acquisitions editors evaluate everything that is submitted to the publisher and identify the books that are right for them to publish. They also make calls to authors and agents that they know to see if there is anything in progress that they may want to buy.

Copy Editor/Proofreader

Copy editors take the completed manuscript and check it for spelling, grammar, and punctuation. They also make sure the-book or story flows in a logical way, that the writing is on the

CHECK IT OUT

See what some celebrities from the worlds of sports, movies, music, and television list as their favorite books at http://www.nea .org/readacross/ resources/celebooks .html.

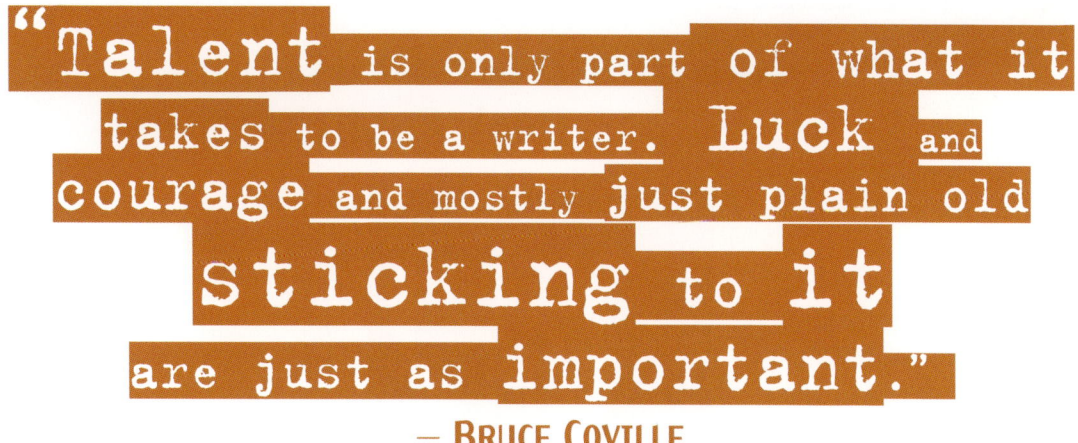

"Talent is only part of what it takes to be a writer. **Luck** and **courage** and mostly just plain old **sticking to it** are just as **important."**

— BRUCE COVILLE
(*I WAS A SIXTH GRADE ALIEN*)

right reading level for the intended audience, and that the author has used a style of writing that goes with other similar books published by the same company.

Copyright Attorney

According to the U.S. Copyright Office, copyright is a form of protection granted to the authors of original works including books, stories, plays, and poems. That means that no one can use anything you have written without giving you credit for it. Copyright attorneys work with authors to make sure that their rights are protected, and that no one misuses an author's ideas or copies their words in other publications without proper permission.

Cover Artist

You've probably heard the saying that you can't judge a book by its cover. The truth is that the cover is one of the biggest factors in people's judgments about whether they want to buy a certain book. The cover artist works with the art director to create a cover that will stand out in a bookstore display, look good in an advertisement, and convey some of the feeling of the book itself. The art that the cover artist creates is much more than a simple drawing. It is usually much larger than an actual book, and can be done in paint, pencil, collage, or on a computer.

NAME: Jennifer Prost

OFFICIAL TITLE: Book Publicist

What do you do?

As a book publicist I work with authors and publishers, trying to get attention for their books. My job is to get the books reviewed in newspapers and magazines and to get the authors interviewed on television, in radio, in print, and on the Internet. I also help set up events like book signings and readings at bookstores.

A publicity campaign for a book can start six months before the book is actu-

ally available in bookstores. Advance copies of the book, called bound galleys, are often printed up and sent to magazines and book review editors and to bookstores where we'd like to set up events. That way some people can get an early look at the book and commit to running a review or schedule the author for a television interview or event. Shows like the *Today Show* and *Good Morning America* and magazines that come out only once a month (like *Glamour*, *Esquire*, and *Vanity Fair*) need lots of time to make decisions about what they want to cover, so they need those bound galleys as soon as possible.

As the publicist, sometimes I accompany authors on their interviews. I get to go to the TV studio and sit with the other guests in the "green room" where guests wait for their turn to be interviewed. I've sat with movie stars, politicians, and dog trainers in the green room! I've also been right on the set while the authors have been interviewed.

How did you get started?

The summer after I graduated from college I participated in the six-week summer Publishing Institute at New York University, one of several such programs around the country. I learned all about book and magazine publishing and met people who played many different roles in publishing. The program helped me realize that publicity was more appealing to me than editorial.

My first job was with a small publisher in Washington, D.C., as a publicity and subsidiary rights assistant and I worked my way up. After seven years, I became the publicity director of a small publishing company and today I own my own public relations firm, specializing in publicity for books.

Designer

Designers determine the way a book looks, its readability, and general appeal. Designers select the typeface (or font), determine how words and illustrations fit together on each page, the design of the chapter headings, and so on. Computers make the designers' jobs much easier and allow for much greater creativity than in times past.

Editor

Editors sometimes start with an idea for a book and then look for an author who can write it. They work with authors to do whatever is possible to make the book better. Editors may suggest a title, rearrange chapters, rewrite sections, and oversee the designer and illustrator. The editor is also the person who gets the sales people excited about selling the book to bookstores.

Illustrator

Illustrations can make a book more interesting or help explain what the author is saying. For children's books, the illustrations may be the heart of the book itself. Illustrators often start with "dummies" of their books–small versions with page-by-page sketches. The illustrations for many books are works of art themselves. Like cover art, they can be done in paint, pencil, collage, or on a computer.

Indexer

Almost every nonfiction book (including this one that you are reading right now) has an index in the back, an arrangement of entries that helps readers find exactly what they are looking for in the book. Indexers are people with special training to create these very specific lists. Some indexers work for publishing companies, but most are freelancers who are hired by authors or publishers.

Librarian

One of the important jobs of librarians is "collection development," deciding what books the library should purchase. Librarians use professional magazines and journals that review new books to decide which new books they want to order.

NAME: Marilyn Allen

OFFICIAL TITLE: Literary Agent

What do you do?

I am a literary agent and I own, along with one partner, a literary agency. Our job is to find talented writers and bring them to the attention of publishing companies. We focus on nonfiction books and help the writers develop proposals for their book ideas. The proposal for a nonfiction book usually includes an overview of the book, some sample chapters, and information about what types of people might want to buy the book and what other books might be available that cover the same general topic. When the proposal is ready, we send it to the right editors at the appropriate publishers. We hope to find the right fit and negotiate a publishing contract for our author. We now represent about 100 writers, mostly in the health, business, and cooking categories.

ON THE JOB

How did you get started?

I got started in the business as a bookstore manager in New England. I then became a traveling sales representative, selling books for Warner Publishing to all the bookstores in the Northeast. I eventually was promoted and moved to New York. After many years and several senior jobs in sales and marketing for major publishers, I left publishing to start this literary agency. I love working with writers and learning new things every day.

Literary Agent

Literary agents are specialists who know what publishers are appropriate for different types of books. They help authors prepare their proposals so that editors will pay more attention to them and they help authors get the best deal from the publisher.

Managing Editor

The managing editor is an extremely organized person who sets up a schedule for the production of each book, coordinates every part of the book production, and makes it all happen on time.

Production Manager

The production department turns the book into a reality. They find the best printers, paper, and cover materials. They oversee the printing process and, when the print run (correct number of books) is complete, take care of shipping them to stores and libraries.

Public Relations Specialist

Public relations (PR) is very important to a book's success. When "everybody" is talking about the next book that you "have to read," it's usually because the PR person was successful in getting the book talked about on television or radio or written about in newspapers or magazines. PR people also set up author visits to schools or local bookstores, and send copies of new books for review to professional journals and magazines.

NAME: Steve Meltzer

OFFICIAL TITLE: Executive Managing Editor

ON THE JOB

What do you do?

I make sure that authors and illustrators deliver their work on time, and that editors, designers, and production people stay on schedule. I watch the cost of producing our books, so that we stay profitable. I supervise the copy editors who, in addition to their other duties, have to make sure that everything is consistent (e.g., if a girl has mole on her right arm on page 3, she should not have a mole on her left arm on page 5). I keep check of all the production stages of a book. I also make sure that sales and marketing understand what the editors think is important about each book, and make sure the sales reps have the materials they need to get the orders.

How did you get started?

I never planned to go into publishing. After college, I visited my sister in New York City and decided to stay for the summer. I ended up as an inventory analyst for a publishing company. After 20 years I have been in several different positions including operations, sales, and acquisitions. I became a managing editor in the late 1990s.

NAME: Tamara Mays

OFFICIAL TITLE: Senior Editor

What do you do?

I work with the I Can Read! books. These are books for kids who are just learning to read. Some of our titles include *Biscuit*, *Amelia Bedelia*, and *Danny and the Dinosaur*. When I look for new books for the list, I have to think about what makes a good I Can Read! book. Are the sentences simple? Does the art help the reader figure out the words? Once I decide I want to get a title, I look at the list and figure out a good time to publish it. Then I have to do some paperwork and present the book in a couple of meetings. If I convince my bosses that this title will be successful, I get to make a deal with the author or her agent.

Then I edit the book. I may change some words to make sure they are easy for kids to sound out. Sometimes I ask the author to make some changes too. Once we have an artist signed up to illustrate the book, I get to see the sketches and then the final art. I work closely with a designer, who makes suggestions about the art. The art and the text are put together on paper the first time in big sheets called mechanicals. I check them for mistakes, and I think about whether there are changes that would make the book better. Besides working on original stories, I also work on movie tie-ins. That is fun because I get to find out about the movie before almost anybody else. I am sworn to secrecy not to tell anything about the plot! Another big part of my job involves getting the books ready to sell. I write a description of each title for the catalog. I also have to present my titles to the sales team. I try to get them excited about selling my titles.

How did you get started?

Many editors go to college where they take some publishing courses, and do internships at publishing companies to get experience and start meeting people in the profession. I didn't do those things. I ran a bookstore for many years. Then my company offered me a job as a children's book buyer. After that I worked for a school book club, which led to my first experience as an editor.

Research Assistant

Research assistants double-check all the facts in nonfiction books. What happens if things are not accurate? At the very least, it can be embarrassing to have some basic facts wrong. Mistakes can be dangerous in a book of science experiments, a health book, or even a cookbook. And mistakes can lead to big legal trouble if the book says something about someone that is not true.

Retail Salesperson

From the big chains, like Borders and Barnes & Noble, to the few remaining independent bookstores, there is always a need for employees to sell books. Stores want salespeople who can make recommendations to customers, suggest what other books they might like, and know something about the latest books that have come out. It's the perfect place for a book lover to be.

Rights and Permissions Manager

The rights and permissions manager is the person who gives other writers permission to quote from your book, and makes sure that you get the credit for it. Did you know that rights and permissions managers also help your book (and you) make more money? A big part of their job is to sell the rights for things like publishing your books in other countries, licensing characters you have created in your books to be on T-shirts or lunchboxes, and adapting your work for movies, television, or Web sites.

Sales Person

Publishers need many different types of sales people to get the biggest possible audience for each book. Trade sales get the books into bookstores. Mass merchandise sales get the books to other retailers, such as Wal-Mart or Target, and to supermarkets. Special sales get the books into catalogs and to specialized stores, like getting your dog-training book into pet shops.

CHAPTER 6

Kids Ask, Authors Answer

You probably have a lot of questions about what it's really like to be an author. The kids in Ms. Yarren's fifth grade class at Northeast School in Stamford, Connecticut, certainly did. After reading all kinds of books and even writing some of their own, they wanted to know more about how the pros do it. And who better to ask than some real-life authors who have definitely been there and done that for many books and many years.

R.L. Stine has been a professional writer for more than 30 years. You probably know him from his series like Goosebumps, Fear Street, and The Nightmare Room. He has been recognized by the *Guiness Book of World Records* as the best-selling author in America and has written more than 300 books in all.

Bonnie Bryant has written more than 100 books in the past 25 years. Have you read anything from The Saddle Club series? Those are just some of the books she wrote as either Bonnie Bryant or B.B. Hiller.

Sue Macy has been writing nonfiction books for almost 15 years. She likes to write about sports, her very favorite topic, and about strong, successful women, her second favorite topic.

CHECK IT OUT

Find out more about these authors on their Web sites:

R.L. Stine: http://www.rlstine.com

Bonnie Bryant: http://www.saddleclubtv.com/bonnies_page.asp

Sue Macy: http://www.suemacy.com

"I knew when I was nine I wanted to be a writer."

—R.L. STINE, AUTHOR

Ms. Yarren's fifth grade class.

R.L. Stine

Did you like to write when you were a kid?

–Christopher K.

R.L. Stine: I started writing when I was nine years old. I found an old typewriter and began banging out short stories and little joke magazines. I couldn't stop. My mother was always trying to get me to go outside and play. But I'd say, "It's boring out there," and just keep on typing. I knew when I was nine I wanted to be a writer.

Bonnie Bryant: I always loved to read; I always loved to write. I started a magazine with a friend in fifth grade. I won an essay contest in eighth grade. I wrote for the newspaper all the way through college.

Sue Macy: I loved to write when I was a kid. It made me feel powerful to be able to use words to create a world and tell a story

How did you get started as an author?

–Steve L., Rachelle J., Ryan D.

R.L. Stine: After college, I moved to New York and started getting writing jobs at magazines. I wrote for all kinds of magazines: movie star magazines, horror stories–even a soft drink magazine! Then I got a job at Scholastic and started writing for kids' magazines. I've been writing for kids ever since–over 30 years!

Bonnie Bryant: I never thought I'd be an author. I didn't believe I was good enough or smart enough. I thought the next-best thing would be to work with authors, especially authors of children's books. So, I worked at a literary agency and then at a publishing company, but I was doing the business stuff –working with contracts, rights, and subsidiary rights.

One night, I dreamt a story and when I woke up in the morning, I remembered most of it and put it on paper. I showed it to a friend at the publishing company where I worked. Three days later, she called me and said, "Bonnie! You're a writer!" I've been writing ever since.

Sue Macy: It seems I've always been writing. I was editor in chief of my junior high school newspaper and my high school newspaper, and I worked at our local paper summers during high school and college. After college, I got a job as a researcher and then an editor at Scholastic, working on their sixth-grade news magazine. In my spare time, I wrote free-lance articles for other magazines. After a while, I realized I wanted to write a book, instead of just short articles.

Why did you decide to write fiction or nonfiction?

–Sara M., Gavin W., Saul S.

Bonnie Bryant: I chose to write fiction because I like making things up. In real life, nothing ever goes exactly the way I plan it; the weather doesn't stay dry for picnics, friends aren't free for a visit when I invite them, and even my children don't always do what I want (imagine that!). When I'm writing, whatever I want to happen, I can make happen in my make-believe universe and I'm finally the boss of the whole world!

Sue Macy: I think I ended up writing nonfiction because much of my early writing experience was as a reporter. I like to hunt down the facts and make sense out of the chaos of real life.

What is it like to be an author?

–Jesus A., Brian B.

R.L. Stine: I love working at home and not having to go back and forth to work. I love sitting and dreaming up new ideas. And mainly, I love all the great mail I get from kids who enjoy my books. That has to be the best part of being an author.

Bonnie Bryant: One great thing about being an author is that you can do it in your pajamas. When I'm at work, nobody but my cat knows what I'm wearing–and she's not telling.

Sue Macy: The best part about being an author is the freedom to explore a subject and tell its story from your own point of view. I love doing research–I feel like a detective, digging through dusty books on library shelves or searching obscure sites on the Internet to get the answers to my questions.

Is it sometimes boring to write for hours and hours at a time?

–Courtney K., Jeremy S.

Bonnie Bryant: Writing is a lonely job. Nobody can do it for you or really help, though I never hesitate to call a friend if I can't think of the right word or fact that I want to include.

Sue Macy: Sometimes writing is harder than other times. But I know that if I just write a certain amount each day, I will finish the book. The best days are those when you're so involved in your writing that time seems to fly. When you finally look up from your computer screen, it's 6:30 p.m. and time to make dinner. But my time isn't just spent writing. As I write, I do more research to answer new questions that come up.

Bonnie Bryant

How do you get your ideas?

–Christopher K.

R.L. Stine: My ideas came from two sources: my memory and my imagination. I try to think back to what I was afraid of or what was scary to me, and try to put those feelings into books.

So many kids ask me this question that I wrote a whole program about how to get story ideas. You can read it in the "teacher" section of my Web site: http://www.rlstine.com.

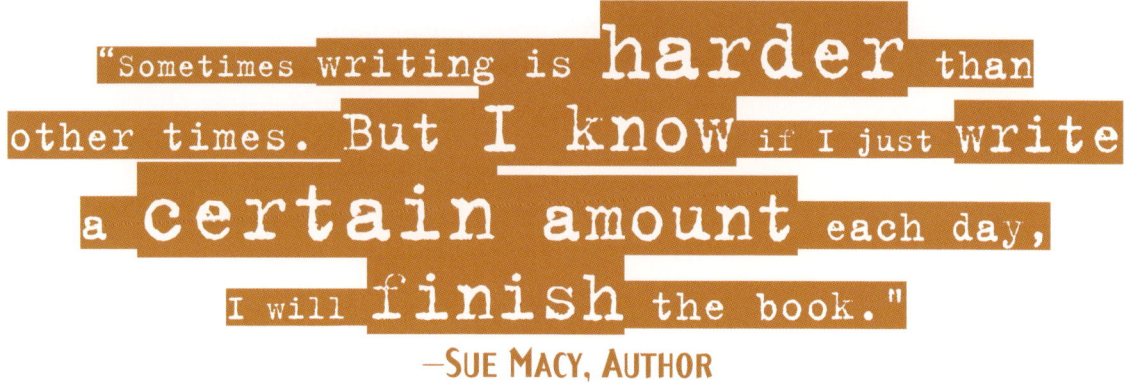

"Sometimes writing is harder than other times. But I know if I just write a certain amount each day, I will finish the book."
—SUE MACY, AUTHOR

Bonnie Bryant: I get my ideas from everywhere. I draw on something that happened when I was a girl, or that happened yesterday at the supermarket. I've taken things that I've seen in magazines and newspapers, things that I've seen happen in my own children's lives, conversations I've overheard on the street, something that someone tells me. I've picked up one of my horse books and flipped through it until I found something I thought was particularly interesting and then wrote a book about it. I've even called my doctor and told him I needed an interesting disease to include in a story.

Sue Macy: Sometimes people suggest book ideas to me, and I do a little research on the subject and then decide whether or not I want to do the book. Other times, however, the book ideas are my own. They often come from things I read in books, magazines, the newspaper, or on the Internet.

How do you actually write a book?

–Hayley S.

R.L. Stine: First, I think of a title. I cannot start writing a book unless I know the title. I also have to know the ending. Once I know the ending, I can figure out how to fool kids and keep them from guessing the ending!

I do a complete chapter-by-chapter outline of every book before I start to write it. That's when I do all the thinking—all the hard parts. Then I can relax and enjoy writing the book.

Bonnie Bryant: The direction for a book can come from lots of different places. Sometimes I have an event I want to write about, for instance, an overnight camping trip, or a horse show. Sometimes I want to introduce a new character or a new skill, or to say something I think is important. Or I might see a picture and know that it would make a good cover and I build a story from that. Many times, I get an idea for a title, or challenge myself by thinking up a silly title and then see if I could build a story under it. Both *Horse Feathers* and *Chocolate Horse* started that way.

Once I know where I'm starting, I need to know where I'm going. For my Saddle Club books, I decide on the plot and a sub-plot. Then I write an outline, which I think is the most important thing I do. My outlines are about 25 pages long, and very thorough. They describe each chapter and what happens so that when I begin writing, I know exactly what I have to cover, the ideas I need to introduce, and the things that have to happen.

Sue Macy: Once I have the research, I make an outline for the book and figure out the lineup of chapters. Then I make folders to hold the research for each chapter. When I start writing a chapter, I list the main topics or events I want to cover. As I write about them, I take them off the list. If I get to the end of the chapter and I've forgotten to include something, I either go back and add it or decide it's not necessary.

"The **fastest** I ever wrote a book was **four days.** The slowest: well, I'm into my **second year** on one **right now.**"
—BONNIE BRYANT, AUTHOR

How long does it take to write a book?

–Joely M., Emily B.

R.L. Stine: It usually takes about two weeks to write a book, once the outline is right.

Bonnie Bryant: That's a hard question! Sometimes the parts of a book can wander around in my brain for a year or more before they start to come together in any useful way. Once I start writing, the process moves quite quickly. I have very tight deadlines, so I usually do the writing in three to four weeks. I can't write a book every three to four weeks. It's too tiring and draining. The fastest I ever wrote a book was four days. The slowest: well, I'm into my second year on one right now.

Sue Macy

Sue Macy: Because I was a magazine editor for a long time, I write like an editor and I revise as I write. Some authors are more comfortable just getting down the story in the first draft and then going back and fixing the language, but that's not me. It's a good day if I write 300 words (three or four long paragraphs) by dinnertime. Between researching, finding the right photographs, and writing, it takes me about nine months to a year to write a book.

How do you come up with the characters for your books? How do you name your characters?

–Gavin W., Hayley S., Jonathan R.

R.L. Stine: For the Goosebumps books, I got all the characters' names from my son's school directory. Most of the kids

"I seldom do **research. It all comes from my twisted mind!**"
—R.L. STINE

in his school got into a Goosebumps book. Sometimes kids win contests to be a character in one of my books. Most of the time, I just make up the names—and then give them their own personalities.

Bonnie Bryant: The characters are the single most important part of a story. I try to create characters that have qualities that my readers share, for better or for worse—people they can relate to. An author has to know the characters as well as they know their best friends. I know their personalities so well that I'd know exactly what each of them would say in any situation.

Sue Macy: When you write nonfiction, you're writing about real people and places, so you don't make up character names.

What kind of research do you have to do when you write a book?

–Demetri B., Courtney K.

R.L. Stine: I seldom do research. It all comes from my twisted mind!

Bonnie Bryant: Even fiction writers have to do a lot of research. I knew some things about horses before I started writing The Saddle Club, but nowhere near enough to write a series. The first thing I did was to take lots of riding lessons, and that was fun. I bought reference books about horses so that if I couldn't remember facts, like whether a rider puts the saddle or bridle on first, I could check one of my books. Then I talked to a lot of professional horse people, including a trainer, a cowboy, an equine vet, an EMT at horse shows, a show judge, a show reporter, a woman who runs a wild pony adoption station, young riders, old riders, and everything in between.

Sue Macy: Before I start to write, I spend a lot of time researching. I always try to get a sense of its time and place by talking to people who were part of the story or by visiting sites where the events took place. For my books on the Olympics, I went to the library at the headquarters of the Amateur Athletic Foundation of Los Angeles. For my book on Annie Oakley, I went to Annie's hometown of Greenville, Ohio. I used their library and I spoke to Annie's grandniece, Bess Edwards.

What was your favorite book when you were a child?

–Sara M.

R.L. Stine: I loved horror comics when I was a kid–the more gruesome and disgusting, the better. Then I discovered the stories of Ray Bradbury, and he turned me into a reader.

Bonnie Bryant: *Charlotte's Web* by E.B. White. I think it's still my favorite. After all, it's about friendship and about writing. You can't beat that.

Sue Macy: As a child, I actually read newspapers and magazines more than books. I loved the feature articles in the *New York Times* and in high school I spent summers writing similar articles for my local paper–about things like the most popular names for babies and a fellow who designed Christmas displays for shopping malls.

CHAPTER 7

Virtual Apprentice
AUTHOR FOR A DAY

Ready to take the virtual apprentice challenge and find out what it's like to be a successful author for a day? Try this out on your own or ask your teacher to make this a class activity.

8:00 You need new ideas for book proposals, so you do what everyone always says and "write from what you know." Start by listing five experiences in your life that you can really remember—include anything from truly wonderful to truly awful experiences.

Can you think of a funny or clever title to match each situation? Write them down in a list.

9:00 Get some story ideas going based on those experiences. Stuck? Go back to R.L. Stine's writing program at http://www.rlstine.com/pdf/rl_classroom_kit.pdf. Feel free to use the "facts" of your experience as a launchpad for creating a fictional story. In other words, it's okay to embellish or exaggerate the situation to make the story juicy.

Depending on which method works best for you, either jot down an outline or write a couple descriptive paragraphs about how you might develop your experience into a full-blown idea for a book.

10:00 Check out the book reviewers. Look on-line for reviews of books you have read recently, using Amazon.com or a search engine, such as Google. Do you agree with the reasons the reviewers give for liking or not liking the books? What would you say about them?

Pretend the other reviewer got fired and you have to step in to do their job. Rewrite one of their reviews so that it expresses what you think about the book.

11:00 Get ready for all those interviews you'll have to give when you finally become a famous author. Practice "interviewing" yourself, using the questions kids asked the authors in Chapter 6.

12:00 Lunch! A light one...you don't want to fall asleep at your desk in the afternoon.

1:00 Get your energy up again with a short walk. Look at some ordinary people, activities, and things that you have never really paid attention to before. What stands out about them when you look at them as if you have never seen them before?

2:00 Pick one of the people you saw on your walk, and consider him or her a fictional character for a story you're writing. Make a list of "facts" about that person: appearance, mood, likes and dislikes, why he or she was doing whatever you saw, and so on. Stay away from the obvious—go for interesting and unusual.

3:00 Create an outline for a story using the character you made up. Give him or her a name, a family, and a childhood. What problems will the character face in your story? Get some outrageous suggestions from the name generators at http://www.seventhsanctum.com/index-name.php.

4:00 How important is the name of a book? Look at any list of recommended books—for example TeachersFirst (http://www.teachersfirst .com/read-sel.cfm) or 100 Best Children's Books of the 20th Century (http://www.cattermole.com/page4.htm). Do the titles alone make you want to read—or avoid—any books?

5:00 Cover time! Plan a cover for a book you'd like to write someday. Get inspiration from some of the books on your shelves. Divide them into two groups—the covers you like and the ones you don't. Use markers, colored pencils, or images clipped from magazines to create a mock-up of your cover.

Virtual Apprentice
AUTHOR FOR A DAY: FIELD REPORT

If this is your book, use the space below to jot a few notes about your Virtual Apprentice experience (or use a blank sheet of paper if this book doesn't belong to you). What did you do? What was it like? How did you do with each activity? Don't be stingy with the details!

8:00 LIFE EXPERIENCES: _____
_____
_____
_____

9:00 LIFE STORY: _____
_____
_____
_____

10:00 BOOK REVIEWS: _____
_____
_____
_____

11:00 AUTHOR INTERVIEW: _____
_____
_____
_____

12:00 LUNCH: _____
_____
_____

1:00 WALK AND WATCH: _____
_____
_____
_____

2:00 CHARACTER DEVELOPMENT: _____
_____
_____
_____

3:00 PLOT DEVELOPMENT: _____
_____
_____
_____

4:00 BOOK TITLE: _____
_____
_____
_____

5:00 COVER DESIGN: _____
_____
_____
_____

Count Me In (or Out)

IS EVERY READER A WRITER?

Reading has always been your favorite subject in school. You are convinced that you can write books that are just as good as many of the ones you read. Does that mean you're cut out to be the next big name author? Or is the reality of writing books more than you bargained for?

Find out now. Grab a sheet of paper, a pen or pencil, and see how you respond to these questions. Hold on to your answer sheet. It will be a good thing for you to refer back to as you begin your writing career.

When I have nothing to do on a weekend afternoon, I usually

❑ Curl up with a book, even if it's one I've read before.

❑ Write in my journal.

❑ Go online to see who's available for a chat.

❑ Walk around the block, just to get out of the boring house.

When I have to write a paper for school, I

❑ Procrastinate until the last minute and then bang it out on my computer as quickly as I can.

❑ Write an outline of everything I want to include and then write the paper.

When I've finished writing a paper, I

❑ Put it aside to bring to school.

❑ Spend the rest of the day reading and re-reading it, improving the writing each time.

I really want to be an author because, I

❑ Know that what I have to say can help people.

❑ Am happiest when I am writing.

❑ Think it would be cool to have my name on books all over the country.

Being an author

❑ Is the perfect career for me because:

❑ Makes NO sense because:

_____
_____
_____
_____

Writing a book

❑ Is just like I thought it would be because:

❑ Is different from what I imagined because:

_____
_____
_____
_____

As for a future as an author

❑ I'm ready to start now! Here's what I'm planning to do to make it happen:

_____
_____
_____
_____

❑ Writing a book is not what I thought it would be. Another career that seems better suited to me is:

_____
_____
_____
_____

APPENDIX

More Resources for Young Authors

BOOKS

Fletcher, Ralph. *A Writer's Notebook: Unlocking the Writer Within You*. New York: HarperTrophy, 2003.

Fletcher, Ralph. *How Writers Work: Finding a Process That Works for You*. New York: HarperTrophy, 2000.

Nixon, Joan Lowery. *The Making of a Writer*. New York: Dell Yearling, 2003.

Nobisso, Josephine. *Show; Don't Tell! Secrets of Writing*. Westhampton Beach, New York: Gingerbread House, 2004.

Reeves, Diane Lindsey and Lindsey Clasen. *Career Ideas for Kids Who Like Writing*, 2nd ed. New York: Facts On File, 2007.

PROFESSIONAL ASSOCIATIONS

Society of Children's Book Writers and Illustrators
8271 Beverly Blvd.
Los Angeles, California 90048
http://www.scbwi.org

WEB SITES

Page by Page: Creating a Children's Book
http://www.collectionscanada.ca/pagebypage/index-e.html

Story Writing Tips for Kids
−Presented by Corey Green, Children's Book Author
http://www.coreygreen.com/storytips.html

Kidsreads.com−Authors
http://www.kidsreads.com/authors/authors.asp

The Children's Book Council
http://www.cbcbooks.org/contacts

Teenreads.Com−Author Listing
http://www.teenreads.com/authors

Society of Children's Book Writers & Illustrators
http://www.scbwi.org/links/mem_links.htm

Educational Paperback Association Top 100 Authors
http://www.edupaperback.org/top100.cfm

Additional Authors and Illustrators
http://www.edupaperback.org/bios.cfm

INDEX